PRESS START TO PLAY

First published in 2025 by Andersen Press Ltd.
6 Coptic Street, London, WC1A 1NH
Vijverlaan 48, 3062 HL Rotterdam, Nederland
www.andersenpress.co.uk

2 4 6 8 10 9 7 5 3 1

British Library Cataloguing in Publication Data available.

ISBN 978 1 83913 609 2

Printed and bound in Great Britain by Clays Ltd, Elcograf S.p.A.

PRESS START TO PLAY

Sam Gayton

Illustrated by

Jack Noel

ANDERSEN PRESS

SOMETIMES, YOU JUST GOTTA LEARN THE BUTTONS

sometimes
you just gotta learn the buttons
twist your hand into the right controller crab
so you can run / fly / jump / grab
better

sometimes your trigger finger
doesn't twitch
the way it needs to

sometimes your fumbly thumbs
can't beat the button drums
in any sort of rhythm
that makes sense

sometimes it comes
so slowly
with each stick mis-twist
with each that
instead of this
until there's ache in your wrist

you think
maybe this game
is not for me

but slowly, slowly
SLOWLY
you start to get your grip
start to skip instead of trip
start to dance in digital
gaming lyrical
buttoning poetry electronically

remember this next time
you stare at squiggles on a page
and wait for them to unsquirm
into some sort of word worm

remember this next time
that lace on that shoe won't tie
that step in that dance won't stick
or you aren't able to times table quick

sometimes
you just gotta learn the buttons

A GAME OF MARBLES

(written after learning that the Milky Way is due to collide with a nearby galaxy in several billion years' time)

our world
is a blue white marble
flicked across the galactic table
at super cosmic speeds

but we still don't know
who set us rolling
in the first place
or what exactly
they are playing at

and in five billion years
when the milky way
smashes into andromeda
flinging a trillion marbles
every which way

i wonder if they'll say

'good move, how about a rematch?'

'. . . nah, we should probably clear this all up
before mum gets back.'

WHAT IF?

stories are imagination engines suspending
disbelief until
their mind bending
heart rending endings

stories are
creativity mines
digging up diamonds that shine
with truths that sparkle for all time

stories aren't just
words that we're reading
but dreams we
need to
believe in
a creed of feeling
for every soul that needs some healing

stories are the stars in the night
the sparks that set us alight
so why are they
so hard sometimes to
write?

well actually
to be a jackanory of story

i'm sure the only
words you need to have in your repertory
are these two

and listen
this is just a suggestion
but if you're stuck upon a story ask yourself one
question:

ask 'what if'
that's all i want to say
a 'what if' will gift
you stories all day
and if you'd like to sample
i will give you an example
here are some 'what ifs'
you can take away today

like what if
you ate a dodgy egg salad sandwich
that granted you a power
you could use to your advantage

where you close your eyes and concentrate
harder and harder
until you turn into a scruffy little
baby chihuahua?

or what if something in the multiverse shifted
and suddenly supers like in DC and Marvel
really existed?

what if you were a hero?
and your best mate was a villain?
would you chuck them into
super prison?

or what if this room became a time machine
and took us all back to prehistory
and a t-rex chomped right through the ceiling
which grown-up do you reckon that we're going to
feed him?

or what if suddenly to our surprise
zombies attack, yeah the dead arise
and we lock ourselves into a shopping mall
how are you going to survive it all?

what if the government tried to control ya?
what if the climate turned much much colder?
what if there's a ninja out to get ya?
what if there's a map to buried treasure?

what if you owned a unicorn?
what if you owned a dragon?
what if you owned a genius evil chicken called kevin?

what if babies could talk?
what if sharks could walk?
what if jack never chopped down the giant
beanstalk?

what if an alien?
what if a fairy?
what if your feet turned super hairy?
actually i don't know if that last one works but

a 'what if' is a game you can play and play
like a hen with golden eggs it'll lay lay lay
if you can't get past the stage where you're staring
at the page
then these words will assuage your rage

WHAT IF?

ONE OF MY KEYBOARD KEYS IS BROKEN - A PUZZLE POEM

?

(see if you can solve this poem!)

one of my keyboard keys is broken
but all of the rest work fine
so there is one bit of the alphabet
that i won't be using this time

my poem can be about anything
except and unless it has got
that one in particular letter
my broken-keyed keyboard has not

it seems you can write quite a lot
with twenty-five of twenty-six
in fact, if i hadn't have told you
it might not have even been missed

so which is the one I'm omitting?
it's very much not on this page
maybe you know the answer
if you know it, then i'll be amazed

IT'S ONLY A WEENSY BIT VIOLENT!!!

it's only a weensy bit violent
there's merely a smidgen of gore
there's barely a bit of bloodspatter
only one or two heads rolling over the floor

but the violence is really quite weensy
the slaughter is really quite slight
i'll only be butchering bad guys
in the rare times i get to engage in a fight

i know it says 18 and over
i know it's called CARNAGE: THE SLAYING
but if i see something more
than a weensy bit violent
i could just shut my eyes whilst i'm playing?

BATTLE ROYALE (with thanks to Jay-Z)

switch on
log in
sit down
relax

controller's ready
mum's getting a plate of snacks

me and you
choose login names
i'm DUSTY LEMON
you're FUNKY JANE

watch the countdown tick
we're starting now
it's game night
and this is a
battle royale

100 other players
but when the game's done
there'll be
99 others
i'll be number one

start up
head down
to the island
map

me and you
we're a team
yeah we got
each other's backs

you look for baddies
while I look for
loot

i only find a fishing rod
i need something to shoot!

when suddenly
BOOM
ahh!
we're under attack

someone called
FLUFFY POODLE's
going brap brap brap

so i use my fishing rod
yoink them close

and we team up
and whack them
... and they're toast

84 other players
when the game is done
there'll be 99 others
i'll be number one

we're looting
we're shooting
driving cars
horn tooting

pick up a bazooka
and we start bazookin

FUNKY JANE'S on the sniper
scopin

DUSTY LEMON (that's me)
sees some
others approachin

like ninjas we hide
in the shadows around them
they've no idea
LEMON and JANE surround them

crouch down
shields up
ambush is ready
wait
wait
wait
wait
steady

NOW!

53 other players
when the game is done
there'll be 99 others
i'll be number one

me and FUNKY JANE
play hard cos
YOLO

we team up cos a duo's
much better than solo

we eliminate a player
called FURIOUS DAVE

emote when win
give that loser a wave

the player count is ticking down
to single figures

me and JANE have got aches
in our trigger fingers

only 2 other players
when the game is done
there'll be 99 others
i'll be number one

tiptoe now
inside some house
stealthy as a really super
stealthy mouse

the count on my screen
says two players left
we're nearly at the end
of our royale quest

me and FUNKY JANE
are nearly done
and that's when it hits me
there can only
be
ONE

betrayal comes fast

like a bullet from a rifle
like a sith lord turning
on their old disciple

i barely have time
to turn around

there's a bang
then my avatar
is on the ground

'FUNKY JANE?' i whimper
in my headseat mic

and FUNKY JANE says
'soz babe
a sniper
gotta
snipe'

one other player
and the game is done
i'm with the 99
FUNKY JANE has won

... MUM?
I'M GONNA NEED
MORE
SNACKS

EMOTIONS ONLY GAMERS FEEL

SIBSLAMMED (**sıbslamm'd : verb**)

the mixture of shock and pride you feel when your little brother or sister beats you at a game for the first time

PLAY JÀ VU (/ˌ**pleɪʒɑː ˈv(j)uː/ : noun**)
the unsettling feeling of flicking through your library and finding a completed game that you don't remember ever owning

ONLINE BOY - A SPOOKY POEM

there's a spooky story
don't know if it's real
but it's still pretty chilling
whatever the deal

apparently, there's this
really cool game online
you can play for free
any place
any time

and the game is
whatever you want it to be
puzzle, building, fps
or strategy

whenever you get bored
it gets more entertaining
almost as if
it wants to keep you playing

there's just one rule
written small on the site
you have to stop the game

before it gets to midnight

that's it
nothing bad
log off before twelve
but this one kid
let's call him timmy
couldn't help himself

timmy started playing
at a quarter past nine
he thought
it's fine
i've got loads of time

but the game got him hooked
like a fish on a line
and before he even knew it
it was 11:49

oops
thought timmy
i forgot to stop
let me do this last level
then i better log off
but the next time his eyes
flicker back to the clock
it's midnight

and that's when he hears it
KNOCK
KNOCK

KNOCK KNOCK
it's coming from behind the screen
KNOCK KNOCK
timmy stares
is he having a dream?
KNOCK KNOCK
is the knock what it seems to be?
KNOCK KNOCK
timmy blinks at the LED display
no way
this had to be fake
it's late, maybe he's starting to hallucinate
this has to be a prank
he looks around for a mate
KNOCK KNOCK
his screen flickers
then starts to
CRACK
and
BREAK

timmy backs away
it's 12:01
he should've stopped playing

should've stopped having fun

his heart starts fluttering
stuttering
like it's buffering
his itching eyes must be glitching
can this really be happening?

a hand is coming out
through the screen's black crack
a bone white hand
timmy tries to jump back

too late
it grabs his shirt
and he feels himself go
bit by giga bit
he feels his body upload
timmy's data, timmy's digital,
timmy's turned to code

he streams from his chair
into the cloud, into the air
before he can scream
there's no one even there

silence
and as the screen powers down to black

you can just see the outline of
a boy inside
trapped

now maybe you're thinking
where's his mum
or his dad?
when i stay up too late
one of them gets mad
how's this kid even playing
until twelve o'clock?
no way in my house would i hear that knock

well timmy's mum and dad
were both gamers too
and the night before
they stayed up playing
until 12:02

it's probably just fake
but all the same
i'm gonna go online
i'm gonna find this game
i'm gonna play it myself
don't worry, i'll be fine
i'll definitely log off
at 11:59
won't i?

TURN THAT THING OFF YOU RIGHT BAD MENACE, PART I

TURN THAT THING OFF YOU RIGHT BAD
MENACE

i will do, i swear mum,
i'm gonna, i promise
but i just gotta get past the haunted forest . . .

CONSIDER THIS
YOUR FIVE MINUTE WARNING
IT'S ALREADY LATE AND
YOU'VE GOT SCHOOL IN THE MORNING

DUMBPHONE / SMARTPHONE

a
e
r
i
a
l
plastic plastic plastic plastic
black black LOGO black black
plastic pixel pixel pixel plastic
black pixel pixel pixel black
plastic pixel pixel pixel plastic
black pixel snake pixel black
plastic pixel pixel pixel plastic
black black black black black
button 1 button 2 button 3
plastic plastic plastic plastic
button 4 button 5 button 6
black black black black black
button 7 button 8 button 9
plastic plastic plastic plastic
button * button 0 button #
black black black black black
plastic plastic plastic plastic

curve rim rim rim rim rim rim rim rim rim rim rim rim rim curve
rim glass glass glass glass glass glass glass glass glass glass rim
rim c glass glass glass glass glass glass glass glass glass glass rim
rim a glass glass glass glass glass glass glass glass glass glass rim
rim m glass glass glass glass glass glass thumb smudge glass port
rim e glass glass glass glass glass glass glass glass glass glass zap
rim r glass glass glass glass glass glass glass glass glass glass port
rim a glass glass glass glass glass glass glass glass glass glass rim
rim glass glass glass glass glass glass crack glass glass glass rim
rim glass glass glass glass glass glass crack glass glass glass rim
rim glass glass glass glass glass glass crack glass glass glass rim
curve rim rim volume up down rim rim rim dent rim rim curve

THE THREE YEAR OLDS ARE HAVING A MATCH!

buckle your seatbelt
batten the hatch
the three year olds are having a match!

toss a foam football
on to the pitch
in every single toddler
a switch gets flicked

cuteness: deactivated
ENGAGE MONSTER MODE

instant mayhem
fifty-a-side
every single shoelace untied

every player
running round the ball
kicking turning spinning
it's a kiddie whirlpool

rush goalies running
two-footed tackling
heading in headfirst

madly cackling

what's offside?
don't know don't care
just yeet the ball
way up in the air

total carnage
red card fouls
dribbling feet
dribbling mouths

arlo's doing divebombs
jaina's sweeping legs
someone call the medics
someone call the feds

hana's doing headbutts
connie's playing rubgy
jackson's doing ninja kicks
things are getting ugly

nursery leader paula
dived in to the fray
no one's seen her since
i hope she's okay

a year six gets the ball

tries to do a rabona
the three year olds just flatten him
like a hundred bulldozers

ball comes to me
i take a touch then a gulp
the whole of the pre-school
beats me to a pulp

one hundred little feet
going hack hack hack
like i am the beanstalk
and they're jack's axe

one hundred little feet
toe-punting my shins
they're the bowling balls
my ankles are the pins

'but i'm the referee!' i scream
they don't seem to notice
who's that gnawing at my leg?
my little brother otis

after that, it's all a blur
don't know how i survived
the doctors in intensive care
say it's lucky i'm alive

the game's still going on
no one knows the score
or even if the foam ball
exists anymore

let's play another game next time
like a gentle game of catch
now line up, kiddies, take one of
these charming cricket bats . . .

ohwaitno –

BAD MR BLOCK

i really am just super stuck
i'm staring at the clock
i don't know what to write at all
it's cos of mr block

mr block's a
massive pest
he is this book's
antagonist

(which means he is the enemy
of poets and all poetry)

i try to write – he blocks my brain
he stops the tracks of
my thought train

he's foiling all my
grandest schemes
taken hostage of my
hopes and dreams

my bright ideas
he snatched like gems
and in their place
he's sent his friends

here's mr worthless
who sows fresh doubts
like rows of growing
brussel sprouts

and megaphone neggy
who, on loudspeaker,
says 'this idea stinks'
on repeater

with these lot
inside my noggin
all my thoughts
they've started robbin'

it's very hard to carry on
when all your good ideas are gone

and nothing seems
quite good enough
you just sort of
run out of
stuff to say

GETTING READY FOR SCHOOL IS SUPER BORING UNLESS YOU DO IT LIKE YOU'RE LEVELLING UP

get in that shower!
deploy aqua power!

equip those pants!
+1 defence!

drink that juice!
energy boost!

speedy wee!
that's double XP!

don't spray the seat!
target practice complete!

socks and shoes on!
side quest done!

bacteria! quick!
toothpaste: EQUIP!

yawning? deleted!
lateness? retreated!
level? completed!
morning? defeated!

GOT GOT NEED GOT

(with thanks to Dan Webster and the Sunshine Wizards)

got
got
need
got

want
want
keep
swap

peel
peel
sticky
stick

get
more
quicky
quick

do
chore
get
paid

penny
penny
pound
saved

next
day
go
shop

some to
keep
some to
swap

new
pack
all
miney

open
up
shiny
shiny

ultra
rare
number
one

next
week
play
ground

show
dad
show
mum

big
crowd
standing
round

get the
set
all
done

walk
up
peer
in

got them
all
need
none

kid
with
shiny
tin

bored
now
what
next

new
cards
new
craze

need
some
new
decks

someone
in the circle
says . . .

got
got
need
got . . .

I AM MONOPOLY, DESTROYER OF FAMILIES, ALL SHALL PLAY ME AND DESPAIR!

it's christmas day

we've been playing
for nine hours straight

i owe mum
eighteen grand
for a one night stay
in mayfair

dad's in jail

and I think
my little sister
just swallowed
the boot

RULES ARE ACTUALLY KIND OF FUN?

okay
bear with me on this one
but rules
are actually
kind of
FUN?

i'm not kidding here
imagine football
but gary from orange class
keeps bringing in his rocket launcher from home
loading it with the school football
and blasting it into the goal
at 1000 miles an hour

not cool, gary
you're winning 159–0
and playtime's
not even over yet

without rules
you don't get
the jaw-drop dribbles of messi
the headed perfection of CR7

instead it's just whoever's got
the biggest cannon

and while we all like
a good explosion
once in a while

it'd be boring
if scoring
was always
rule-ignoring

you'd never feel like you
truly WON
trust me on this
rules are actually
kind of fun

oh no they're not

quiet, gary

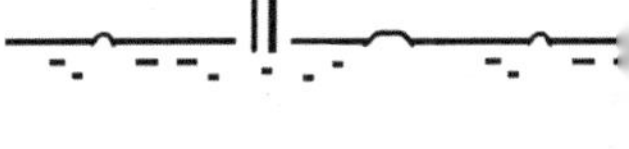

GAMES TO BEAT THE BULLIES

you don't have to keep
trying
and failing
to win the
game
they make
you play

you can take
what lives you have left
get up
walk away
and find someone
who doesn't make you
feel like a loser

trees are good
game buddies, for example

you can
try and catch
the helicopter seeds
a sycamore
is throwing down to you

or toss pebbles
and try to hit the target
of those weird stumpy
things on tree trunks
you know, the ones that look like
buttholes

even do a few rounds
of red light green light
with a local
squirrel

and if none of this
is helping
maybe just
close your eyes
and do the game
where you count
each breath
you take
and know
that this one
no, this one
no, this one
is you
racking up
a new high score
is you being
a winner

HIGH SCORE HOLDER

this is my track
i wrote it to rap
words are my game and
i'm on the attack

i'm a pro
like a minecraft master

words are the blocks that I build with faster

and farther and stronger
and better and longer
think you could beat me?
you couldn't be wronger

i know the cheat codes
i'll beat you with eyes closed
switch it up like nintendo
take your coins just like in mario

i'm the high score holder
you can be pepsi
but i'm coca cola
pressing continue but
this is game over
nah you don't get it i'm just gonna troll yer

like i just told yer

in the battle royale
you can throw in the towel
i'll swipe it to wipe up the sweat
from my brow

throwing shuriken rhyme
like a ninja I climb
to such lyrical heights
when I fight you resign

i wanna be humble
but this is my rumble
my aiming is deadly
my flow don't fumble

up down
look around
right stick
left stick
I rhyme
like I game
and I win
real quick

i'm the high score holder
you can be pepsi

but i'm coca cola
pressing continue but
this is game over
nah you don't get it i'm just gonna troll yer
like i just told yer

TURN THAT THING OFF YOU RIGHT BAD MENACE, PART II

TIME'S UP, SON –

but this level's just begun!

YOU PROMISED –

but my progress!

WELL I'M AFRAID –

but it won't save!

I'M AT MY LIMIT –

just one more minute!

BOSS LEVEL POEM

I AM BOSS LEVEL POEM!
I CANNOT BE BEAT!
WRITE ME FOUR LINES THAT RHYME
OR ADMIT DEFEAT!

rhyming is as easy
as a summer breezy
thank you and pleasey
macaroni cheesy

HMM. NOT BAD.
NOW RHYME EVERY
OTHER LINE

OH – AND ALSO
EACH LINE
CAN'T BE MORE
THAN THREE SYLLABLES
LONG.

LET THE TORTURE
BEGIN!

syllables?
let me count
have to get

the right amount . . .
oh wait, that's four
and so is that – NOOOO!

MWAHAHAHA!
I AM BOSS LEVEL POEM! I –

try again:
three each line
must have three
every time

oh – and they
have to rhyme
is that it?
am i fine?

URRRRGH
TIME FOR
MAXIMUM DIFFICULTY MODE

WRITE ME
A SHAKESPEARIAN SONNET
WITH ONOMATOPOEIA

AND SUPER SOPHISTICATED VOCAB
I MEAN
REALLY MASSIVELY LONG WOW WORDS

LIKE
FIDUCIARY RESPONSIBILITY

AND YOU HAVE TO SAY STUFF LIKE
'THOU ART'

AND
UM
UM

AND
SIMILES

HELLO?

hi?
sorry
who dis?

THIS IS
BOSS LEVEL POEM!
I CANNOT BE BEAT!
WRITE ME A POEM
OR –

oh, it's you
you're still here?

OF COURSE I AM!
WHY AREN'T YOU WRITING?!

well
it kind of got a bit
not much fun
didn't it?

FUN?
POETRY ISN'T
MEANT TO BE
FUN!
IT'S
VERY, VERY SERIOUS

well
i suppose
that's sort of why
i stopped doing it

OH.
I SEE.

maybe
if you made it
a bit more fun, then
i might want to
start again?

FUN?
OKAY.
HOW DO I DO THAT?

well
why don't we just
try and
make each other laugh?

FINE.
FIRST ONE TO SMILE LOSES!
BOSS LEVEL POEM WILL DESTROY –

no, no, no
there's no loser

NO LOSER?
IF THERE'S NO LOSER,
HOW DO YOU WIN?

you don't win
you just have to
let your words
play

okay?

. . .

. . .

. . .

. . .

OKAY.

SHMOKAPON - GOTTA KEEP CATCHIN'

shmokapon!
shmokapon!
it's cool
you catch them one by one!
i've no idea what's going on
but i'll join in cos it's
SHMOKAPON!

what is this craze?
it's too complex
just let me check
my shmokadex

there's pinkerchu
and bogeysaur
and biggly jeff
and dumbledore
and teenage turtle
i think he's one
i'm pretty sure
they're shmokapon

you've got all kinds of
shmokatypes

a smorgasbord of
shmoka lifes
there's jomblypom
and wigglybutt
evolving from
the jabbahutt

there's mr ketchup
kanga-fuey
shmeedle-fadeedle
bingo-bluey

my mate just got a fruitymax
when his mum bought him
some shmokapacks

with shmokamon
what do you do?
you train them up
to fight for you

you teach them
lots of shmokamoves
like 'ticklyslap'
and 'i'm confused'

and 'dragon toe'
and 'solar dump'

and ‘ultra bouncy castle jump’

i’ve heard word of a legendary
mutant shmokamon
he’s scary

someone said his name was
MOOTOO?
or maybe it was
TOOMOO?
which i think maybe means
that he’s far too much cow to handle

. . . in truth
i don’t know what goes on
with all these cutie
SHMOKAPON

i really wish
i knew the words
to be part of the
shmoka-herds

i just want to be
in the fun
but all my
shmoka-speak
is wrong

so i'll curl up in a
shmokaball
sometimes games are
kind of cruel

THE WORLD WITHIN MY BEDROOM

i'll build a world within my bedroom
where happy pixel people
walk contented circles
through perfect towns

i'll build a world within my bedroom
where i'll always get
another try
where i'll never feel
lost
where all the fighting
has a point

i'll build a world within my bedroom
where no one is
alone
where the monsters are
beatable
where dreams are
achievable

whenever mum tells me
that games are a waste of time
compared to say
my algebra homework

i say, seriously mum?
algebra?
i'm a bit busy
learning how
we make the world
a better place

THE GREATEST GAME EVER MADE

it isn't on XBOX
or PS5
it isn't online
isn't on hard drive

it's TAG
it's IT
it's GOTYA
it's TIGGY

it's CHASE
it's LURGY
it's YOU CAN'T
CATCH ME

it's a game with
many names
you can play it
any way
any day
for forever
or the length
of a lunch play

TAG! TAG! TAG! TAG!
IT! IT! IT!
TIG! TIG!
LURGY!
YOU'RE NEVER GONNA CATCH ME!

who's played TAG
with a little safe space
like a place
when you're chased
you can race
and be safe

it's BASE
it's SAFE
it's LURGY-FREE ZONE

it's IMMUNE
it's TRUCE
it's TIME-OUT
it's HOME

TAG! TAG! TAG! TAG!
IT! IT! IT!
TIG! TIG!
LURGY!
YOU'RE NEVER GONNA CATCH ME!

in the future i think kids
will probably call it
#
or
HYPER CATCH 3000
or
GOING VIRAL
who am i kidding no one's gonna play tag in the future
like we have xboxes now
aint playing no tag
i'm racking up a win-streak in the latest massively online multiplayer
just loading it up actually
wait a second
it's saying it needs to update?
well how long is that gonna take?
fourteen hours?
what am i supposed to play now then?

TAG! TAG! TAG! TAG!
IT! IT! IT!
TIG! TIG!
LURGY!
YOU'RE NEVER GONNA CATCH ME!

understand
we're just tiny little grains of sand
in the grand hourglass of time

yet there'll never be a day
when there's no demand
for a game you can play
tagging people with your hand
and they say
that the universe is still expanding
and tag as a game
will ever be rebranding
demanding
you join in
the tagging and chasing
and running to safe-basing
all over the place and
that's why it's greatest ever game that's been
yeah
let's give it up for tag
hail to the king

TAG! TAG! TAG! TAG!
IT! IT! IT!
TIG! TIG!
LURGY!
YOU'RE NEVER GONNA CATCH ME!

EMOTIONS ONLY GAMERS FEEL, THE SEQUEL

COCOONEA (noun, **kəˈkuːniːə**)
the warm, safe and familiar feeling you have when playing your favourite game

LEVELATION (noun, **ˈlɛvlˈleɪʃn**)
the indescribable triumph of getting past that bit you've been stuck on for weeks

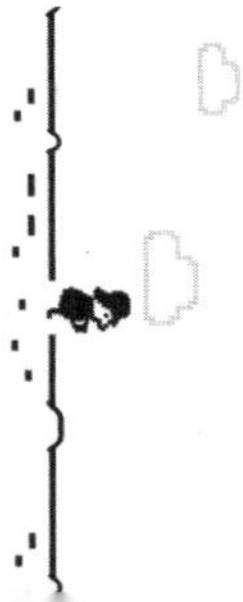

THIS IS WHAT I ACTUALLY DO WHEN I'M GAMING

i play
i have fun
i sneak, jump, dodge, run

i battle
i race
i build and erase

i beat
i get beat
i get used to
defeat

i try
i try again
then i win
in the end

i team
i scheme
i score
i stream

i achieve
i believe
control a guy
called steve

i design
i waste time
i craft
i mine

i explore
i scout
i meet friends
hang out

i circle x square
like
comment
and
share

i travel
i scrabble
i puzzle unravel

i collect
i perfect

tether tech
to
tech

i connect
up the TV
for when you want to
watch netflix

i aim
i train
gain internet fame

i make worlds
cast spells
game with
boys and girls

i level up
i log in
i feel part of
a thing

this is what I actually do when I'm gaming

TURN THAT THING OFF YOU RIGHT BAD MENACE, PART III

FOR THE VERY LAST TIME
YOU MASSIVE SATSUMA

all right mum
i'd have logged off sooner
but I just gotta equip this big ol' bazoomer
does 999 damage
utterly savage
shall I shoot at that dude whose head is a cabbage?

WOW, SON, NICE HEADSHOT!
I MEAN –
STOP
TURN IT OFF
JAMMIES, TEETHIES, PEE PEES
WE CLEAR?

crystal!
i'm just waiting . . .
i think it's
um
updating

WHY OH WHY DO I NEVER SAY UNO?

miss a turn
pick up two
send it back to me
but every round
there's a sound
i forget to speak

i know that it's coming
i know
i know
so why oh WHY
do i NEVER say
UNO

pick up two and wait my turn
it's every time
i never learn

whenever i've got
one card to go
i will never
i mean
NEVER
i just never say
UNO

two in my hand
and i'm on the attack
you tried a pick up 4
but i pick up 4 you back i'm just so eager
to defeat you
that
oh
oh
OH
i just forgot
i just
ah
i just
didn't say
UNO

this time
THIS time
i'm about to win
get ready to play your
tiniest violin

because i'm down to my last card
wait
wait
NOOOOO
i could've
would've

should've
but i didn't say
UNO

okay
okay
focus brain
i WILL NOT
make that
mistake again

i will rise
i will vanquish
this game has just begun –
i will rule supreme at UNO!

huh?
you just won?

THERE'S A GLITCH IN THIS POEM

there's a gl×tch ×n th×s poem
×'ve no ×dea why
somethng we×rd's go×ng on
×t blanks out the

'i'

oh! the i is b×ck
w×it
no w×y
i c×n't write
×nything ×t ×ll
if i don't h×ve ×n

'a'

a works again!
××c×ll×nt!
... a n×w myst×ry
now i'm l×ft h×r× wond×ring
wh×r× is th×

'e'

e's ret×rned!
b×t right on c×e
all of a s×dden
i'm witho×t a

'u'

y×u've g×t t× be j×king
n×w i've n×t g×t
×ne single bl××ming
y×u kn×w what

there's a glitch in the p×em
i've n× idea why
and n×w i can't
st×p
×r even say
g××dbye

WHAT THE WORLD SAYS

how barometric sheets of air
rise and shift
like continental shelves
and bring us blizzards?

snow idea, but –

i know a back garden

of untrod white

is the way the world says

'snowball fight'

how ocean wavelengths
move in sine curve shape
and swell, and swell
and seeming never break
until the beach?

not shore, and yet –

i know that crashing fringe
of foaming tide

is the way the world says

'surfers, ride'

how sprouting shoots
spread networked roots
and branch green roofs
that sieve carbon from our air?

i'll leaf that to

the scientists, although —

i know those tangled arms

of sunlight and time

is the way the world says

'come on, climb'

how any of this works,
this sky
this earth
this sea
this spell of cells that's somehow me?

it's all a

wondrous mystery, except —

i know the whole wide world

just seems to say

in each and all and every part

'come play'

SQUARE MOON

square moon in a screen sky
bathe my eyes in pixel stars
whilst stretching down
beneath my feet
the endless
algorythmic deep

this one and zero universe
this infinite no-sided sandbox
this world that's held
in a machine
the way a head
might hold a dream

we can make anything here
raise monuments to youth and fun
soar and swoop
like icarus
mod the fabric
of existence

most evenings, though
it's more fun to chill out
and in each other's ears make
fart noises

TURN THAT THING OFF YOU RIGHT BAD MENACE, PART IV

NICE MUM MODE IS OVER, GIMME THAT CONTROLLER.

sure thing, mum! just aim for that boulder –
ah
too bad
you got got by that soldier

WHAT? I DID? NO FAIR.

yeah...
you should've pressed circle instead of square . . .
. . . wanna try again?

UM.
ALL RIGHT. JUST ONE TURN.
BUT THEN BED. LIKE I SAID.

GAMES I PLAYED

i played a game
when i was ten

called 'stand on a pitch
and pretend you like football'

i played a game
when i was twelve

called 'never tell anyone
you like pretty jewellery'

i played a game
when i was fifteen

called 'how long can you
hide your love for
craig david?'

i was pretty good
at those games

racked up a ten year winstreak
against myself

VCR DEMON

VCR tape
stacked there on a shelf
in a charity shop
for mental health

obsolete format
no one wants to buy
which is good
because if you were to watch it
you would probably
die

you see
back in the 90s
a demon from hell
chose to make this tape
his home
in the mortal realm

tech has moved on
left him behind
but the demon's still there
trapped in rewind

spare a thought for all the demons trapped
in utterly obsolete
formats

walkman tape
and floppy disc
CD, cartridge, betamax

STEALING AINT THIEVING IN WRITING

you might think you're original
sorry
nah
nope
whatever what if you can riff has been done no
joke
every story has been told by some old dead
bloke
with a name like william shakespeare
man i can't even cope

but hold up
wait a sec
here's the big reveal
here's the twist in the tale
where the beans get spilled
here's the dark before the dawn
here's the lips unsealed
if nothing is original
you have to steal

so get ready to heist
get ready to thieve

best believe we're gonna find what your story needs
cos stories are like banks
filled with dollar notes
except the notes are ideas
ideas called

TROPES

stealing
aint thieving
cos in writing, you take a trope from the genre

so what's a trope?
well . . .

a trope is something we've seen
in a story before
like a haunted house with a creaky door
or an evil dude in a hooded cloak
yeah all that stuff and more
we call a
TROPE

and a genre is just a trope collection
like fantasy
spy thriller
sci fi

and western
and some I find fun
and some just bore me
but here's the thing
they're mostly all
ONE STORY

stealing
aint thieving
cos in writing, you take a trope from the genre

what story you say?
well, it's called
'the hero's journey'
and this is how we do it

so first I need a hero
someone starting from a zero
maybe their mum and dad are missing
it's a bit unclear though

and they've got some super power
but they don't even know
until one day they get a mission
and they have to go

take the ring
use the force

gather the stones
go to hogwarts
save the kingdom
slay the beast
get the black pearl
find the golden fleece

stealing
aint thieving
cos in writing, you take a trope from the genre

but no hero's alone
when they do their quest
no it's best if they're blessed
with a helpful guest
like a teacher who can feature
with a hero test
usually a bearded grandad is best

stealing
aint thieving
cos in writing, you take a trope from the genre

and then you need a friend
who'll stay true to the end
when the hero needs a hand
they've got a hand to lend

and through thick and thin
when the walls cave in
at the bitter end
the friend
will still be there, helping

stealing
aint thieving
cos in writing, you take a trope from the genre

but don't start writing yet, all you story thieves
there's one final trope, all stories need
i'm talking about the ominous entity
the shadow with this mad bad energy

giving it 'MWA HA HA'
giving it 'MY PLAN IS COMPLETED'
giving it 'DARKNESS, RISE'
giving it 'I CANNOT BE DEFEATED'

and sometimes this evil villain
has millions of minions
and the whole world is fallen
beneath their deadly dominion

and for all the hero's brilliance
their resilience is fading and they're failing

cos the fight is so much harder
than training

and they're saying
'i just can't'
as the villain's supreme
and then just at the end of the final fight scene –

grab the sword
raise the wand
feel the force
go to infinity
and beyond

and the villain goes NO
but it's a NO that's long
like NOOOOOOOOOOO
and then they're gone

stealing
aint thieving
cos in writing, you take a trope from the genre

you've seen it
you've heard it
it's all the same journey
but just before jk rowling goes and gets her
attorney

every hero starts from zero
then achieves the glory
and no matter how many times you have heard
this story
yeah no matter how many times
it's all been done
the glory of stories is –
they're still fun

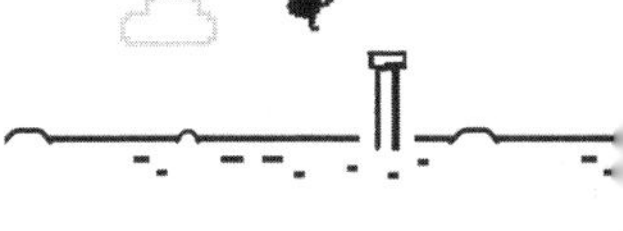

THE CHICKEN OF INSPIRATION

i am the idea chicken
i'm not pulling your leg
i lay inspiration
in the form of an egg

i am the idea chicken
this is no joke
my yolks are eurekas
for day-dreaming folk

i am the idea chicken
this is not fake news
i'm the source of all stories
i'm the one true muse

i lay the best laid plans
i hatch all the plots
i crack every mystery
from hardboiled to not

i incubate inspiration
my butt's an idea oven
if you ever need a 'what if?'
i've got them by the dozen

for i AM the idea chicken
and cos i spoil you rotten
you can watch me hatch a fresh idea
from out of my bottom

first i cock my wings out
buck buck buck buck buck
then i give a big BUCAW
just for luck

ruffle up, settle down
shake my tail feather
some ideas come super quick
some seem to take forever

sometimes, i sit and sit and sit
and sit and sit and sit
luckily we chickens are given to sittin'
we're super good at it

then suddenly, out of nowhere
just like magic
here it is!
a love fresh brand new idea
will suddenly

— just like that —

APPEAR!

B
U
C
A
A
A
A
A
WWWWW!

sorry about that.
sometimes it needs a bit of pushing at the end

here it is!
so beautiful!
a perfect, single
idea oval

and with it, I know what to do
i'm going to give it
to (you guessed it) YOU!

(don't worry if you're quite a crowd . . .
idea eggs are imaginary
sharing's allowed)

ready . . . catch!
it's yours now – take good care of it

it might just hatch a baby chick . . .

isn't that just fingerlickin'?
now we all have our own
inspiration chicken

POETRY IS VERY HARD AND I AM STUCK

roses are red
the stars are a glowin'
it's taken me ages
to think of this poem

LET'S MAKE A MONSTER

let's make a monster
let's make a monster
horn of a unicorn
claws of a lobster

let's build a beast
let's build a beast
ten arms
ten legs
ten heads at least!

think you're the hero?
wrong: you're the feast . . .

stuck on a story? just add in a beast
it's a technique that's worked since the ancient
greeks at least
you take two animals
mix them up together
instantly it makes a
story much better

a troll inside a cave
dragons on treasure
you can make a monster
cute or gory or whatever so

let's make a monster
let's make a monster
horn of a unicorn
claws of a lobster

let's build a beast
let's build a beast
ten arms
ten legs
ten heads at least!

think you're the hero?
wrong: you're the feast . . .

the hippogriff
the harpy
and the manticore
the mermaid
the medusa
and the minotaur
the beasts that medieval map-makers used to draw
of what the sailors saw
beyond the farthest shore
there are beasts that soar
there are beasts that roar
and there are beasties that will bite you with tooth and claw

and we could probably make a million more
but now it's time to do a bit that you have heard
before . . .

let's make a monster
let's make a monster
horn of a unicorn
claws of a lobster

let's build a beast
let's build a beast
ten arms
ten legs
ten heads at least!
think you're the hero?
wrong – you're the feast . . .

TURN THAT THING OFF YOU RIGHT BAD MENACE, PART V

mum, i'm tired
can I please go to sleep?

YEAH, SON, YEAH, SOON AS THIS LEVEL'S
COMPLETE

please mum
i just wanna do my teeth . . .

CIAO CIAO NOOBIE!
BAZOOMERED IN THE FACE!
MUM THE DESTROYER GETS ANOTHER
FIRST PLACE!

SECOND HAND GAME SHOP

dusty retro consoles
chunky button controls

battered scratchy game discs
broken stepped-on cases

rainbow wire bird's nest
bundles up for purchase

CDs and cartridges
high scoring my happiness

piled packs of old plastic
simply fantastic

cybernetic treasure
i can look through at my leisure

all this awesome stuff
other people got rid of

the dude up at the counter
lets me look for hour after hour

and though it looks like junk
antiquated and defunct

i just think you are the top
second hand game shop

I WISH TODAY HAD BEEN A GAME

i wish today had been a game
so i could turn it off and on again

and start from yesterday's save point

if today had been a game
i could've let my best mate
take over my controller
as i sat there on the sofa

eating crisps until he won

if today had been a game
matt johnson
would've been an NPC
and i could've played as
someone other
than
me.

if today had been a game
after school at the park
would've been a cutscene
i could skip

by holding down start

today had no cheat code
or easy mode
no reload, no save

and i'm scared
that i'm going to have to replay
the same today
tomorrow

GREG'S TINY ARMY

greg at school
is not that cool
in fact he's sort of goofy

but no one's ever
mean to him
due to his tiny army

see greg's got little
figurines
he says they are called
space marines

a soldier glued on
to a stand
that greg has brushed
with greenish sand

each one no taller
than your thumb
with chainsaw swords
grenades and guns

greg paints them all
he's really good
like none of us lot

ever could

the dullish gleam
of sharpened steel
the leather boots
it all looks real

the gritted teeth
the buzzcut heads
the armoured fists
the bandaged legs

the eyes with little
pupilled dots
far, far, smaller than
full stops

greg says he uses
eyelashes
dips them in ink
like paintbrushes

i don't think even
georges seurat
could jot a dot
as small as that

eyelash brushes

are kind of barmy
but not if you've a
tiny army

cos as greg says,
how are they gonna fight t'zeench's swarming
horde if they aint got no eyeballs?

greg at school
is not that cool
and way back in the past

some older kids
elbowed his ribs
and tripped him up and laughed

greg spent his lunchtimes
sat in class
he watched the clock
'til quarter past

as kids outside
all larked about
greg got his
tiny army out

and stood each soldier
to attention

like they could give him
some protection

maybe they did
because me (sam gayton)
noticed greg
as he was painting

'super cool!'
'look at that sword –
he's fighting off the
swarming horde!'

at playtimes now
greg still stays in
and i do too
i paint with him

arrange our squads
to fight the hordes
(greg still does
all the eyes of course)

side by side
we play along
that's what makes
greg's army strong

IF INFINITE LIVES ARE A THING

if we had infinite lives
no limit
to our retries
i still probably
wouldn't
skydive

but i would press undo
on the time i put a cactus
on my sister's highchair
and poured purple slime
on my cousin holly's hair

if all our days
could be replayed
i'd go to grave
after grave
after grave
without holding a
tarantula

but i would go see
gramps in the hospice
kiss his grey unshaven cheek

say some of those words
i thought but didn't speak

maybe infinite lives are
not a thing
maybe it's one go then
game over, no
reincarnating

but
what if
after we die
the screen
pops up with a
. . . retry?

i'll click
YES
you choose
CONTINUE

let's meet back here next playthrough
and take a few more regrets
out of this poem

EMOTIONS ONLY GAMERS FEEL, REDUX

PREGRIEF (noun, priːgriːf)
playing something so good that you're already sad for the moment you complete it

THUNGERBOLTED (noun, θʌŋgə:bəʊltɛd)
the sudden shock of coming back to reality after hours of gaming and realising that it's dark outside your windows, you're cold, and you desperately need toast

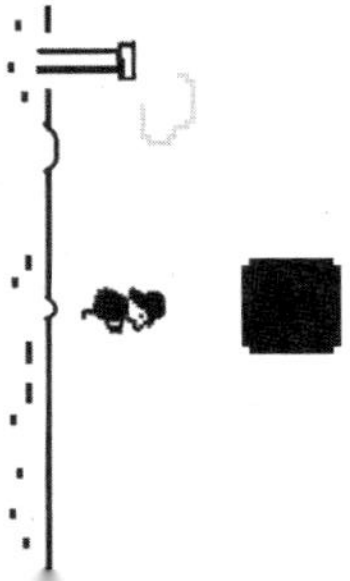

SAM CLICKS QUIT

sam clicks quit. time to play something else
itching tired eyes, he sighs and presses start
the screen goes blue as it resets itself
this game seems a challenge, he's already lost a heart

itching tired eyes, he sighs and presses start
tries and lives counting down, he presses yes to continue
this game seems a challenge, he's already lost a heart
he silent screams into the sofa, back at the menu

tries and lives counting down, he presses yes to continue
what else is there to do on this long afternoon?
he silent screams into the sofa, back at the menu
he puts down the controller, stares out of the room

what else is there to do on this long afternoon?
outside in the garden, his sister kicks a ball
he puts down the controller, stares out of the room
she flicks another header off the back brick wall

outside in the garden, his sister kicks a ball
the screen goes blue as it resets itself
she flicks another header off the back brick wall
sam clicks quit, time to play something else

JOIN?

join in
even if you watch
join in
even if you lose
join in
even if you're trying to act cool
even if this feels too young
you're going to be old for decades
join in and feel young for a second

the words
'join in'
have joy in them
the words
'sitting out'
don't

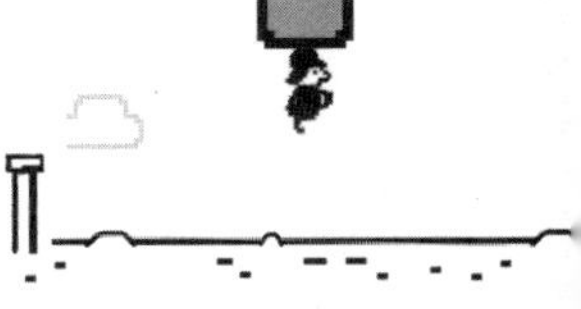

WANT TO PLAY?

PLAY YOUR OWN POEM!

score a point each time
that any two lines rhyme

a point for any imagery
like metaphor or simile

a point for each alliteration
add your score like an equation

can you figure out this poem's score?
bet you can't beat me
bet you can't score more

PLAY YOUR OWN POEM II: FEELINGS EDITION

score one point
each time
your words
cross the space
between me and you
and make us both
feel less alone

a point for each time
you break your own heart

double your score for
mending it back together

a point each time
you try to name
a feeling you can't speak

don't bother
counting your points up
you only win if
at the end of writing the poem

you feel the way you do
after a good cry
lighter

FIND A POEM . . .

you can get poems anywhere
especially in books

first, go to a place with books
like the library
or school

now write down your birthday
done it? easy

first take your birthday month
count that number of books on a shelf

take the book you get to
open it up

next take your birthday day
count that number of pages

take the first words you see
you can have a phrase
or something smaller
but nothing longer than a line

write down the words you've found
and the book you found them from

then do it again
until you've found
a word jumble
like mine

. . . LIKE MINE!

who has laid this enchantment upon the whole land?	(from *The Saga of Erik the Viking*, by Terry Jones)
is that any way for a cop to behave?	(from *Dog Man Unleashed*, by Dav Pilkey)
coming here? with no warning?	(from *Wings of Fire*, by Tui T.Sutherland)
BARB! STAY DOWN!	(from *Barb and the Battle for Balliwick*, by Dan and Jason)
you got so angry you made it RAIN!	(from *Looshkin*, by Jamie Smart)

PRESS START ON POETRY

press start on poetry
unpause that brain
navigate new ways
whatever your username

press start on poetry
just try a tongue twister
set a record win streak
for picking pecks of pickled peppers

press start on poetry
aim at an alliteration
see if that same starting sound
ends in some sort of creation

press start on poetry
do variation next
design rhymes that run in and over
lines to give your text some flex

(that's internal rhyme
and enjambement
by the way)

press start on poetry
get some images in too

grip your pen like it's a sword
strike that paper true

press start on poetry
just repeat if you ever get stuck
repeating isn't cheating
for every goose
there's a
duck
duck
duck

press start on poetry
treat it like a game
a playground for your words
to play again
again
again

BEAT BOXES

each	box	is	a	po
two	beats	get	called	feet
end	each	line	and	take
pause	and	breathe	in	deep
beats	are	made	of	sy
words	they	teach	in	schools
sy	lla	bles	are	buil
poem	just	fill	a	box
one	word	in	one	box
you	might	have a	better	time
squee	zing	words	in	to
faster	means your	poetry		rocks
leave	some	blank		
it	makes	a	poem	
po	ems	are	a	game
let your	ears hear	all	the	mu

em's	beat	it's	weird	but
		/		
some	beats	to	take	a
		/		
lla	bles	(them	bits	of
		/		
ding	blocks	to	play	this
		/		
is	fine	but	mixing it	up
		/		
a	box	means you	say	them
		/		
that's	rhythm	resting	/	
	inter	resting	/	
with	rhythm		/	
sic	in them			listen

NOW TAKE THESE BOXES AND FILL THEM WITH WORD-BEATS!

POEMS ARE LABYRINTHS

LABYRINTH SHEET

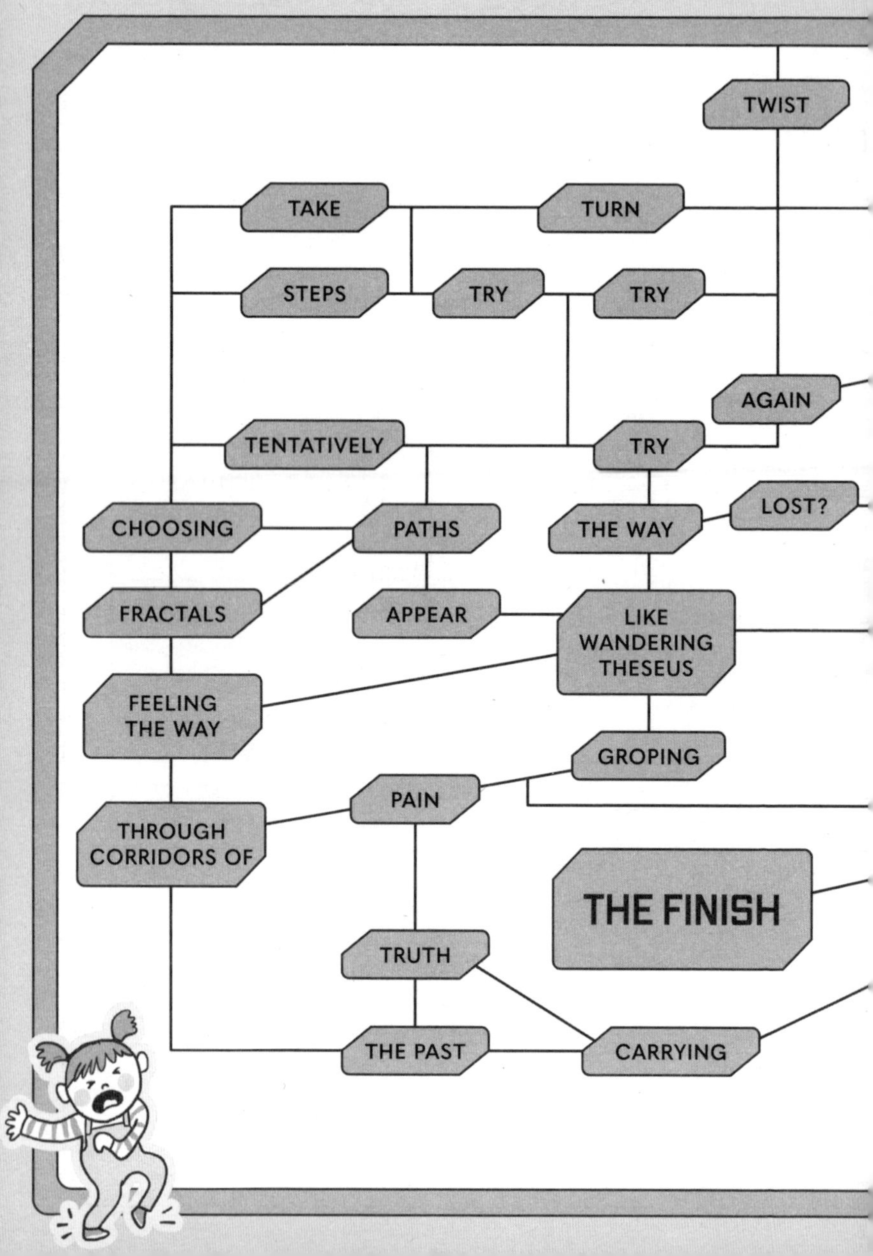
TWIST
TAKE
TURN
STEPS
TRY
TRY
AGAIN
TENTATIVELY
TRY
LOST?
CHOOSING
PATHS
THE WAY
FRACTALS
APPEAR
LIKE WANDERING THESEUS
FEELING THE WAY
GROPING
PAIN
THROUGH CORRIDORS OF
THE FINISH
TRUTH
THE PAST
CARRYING

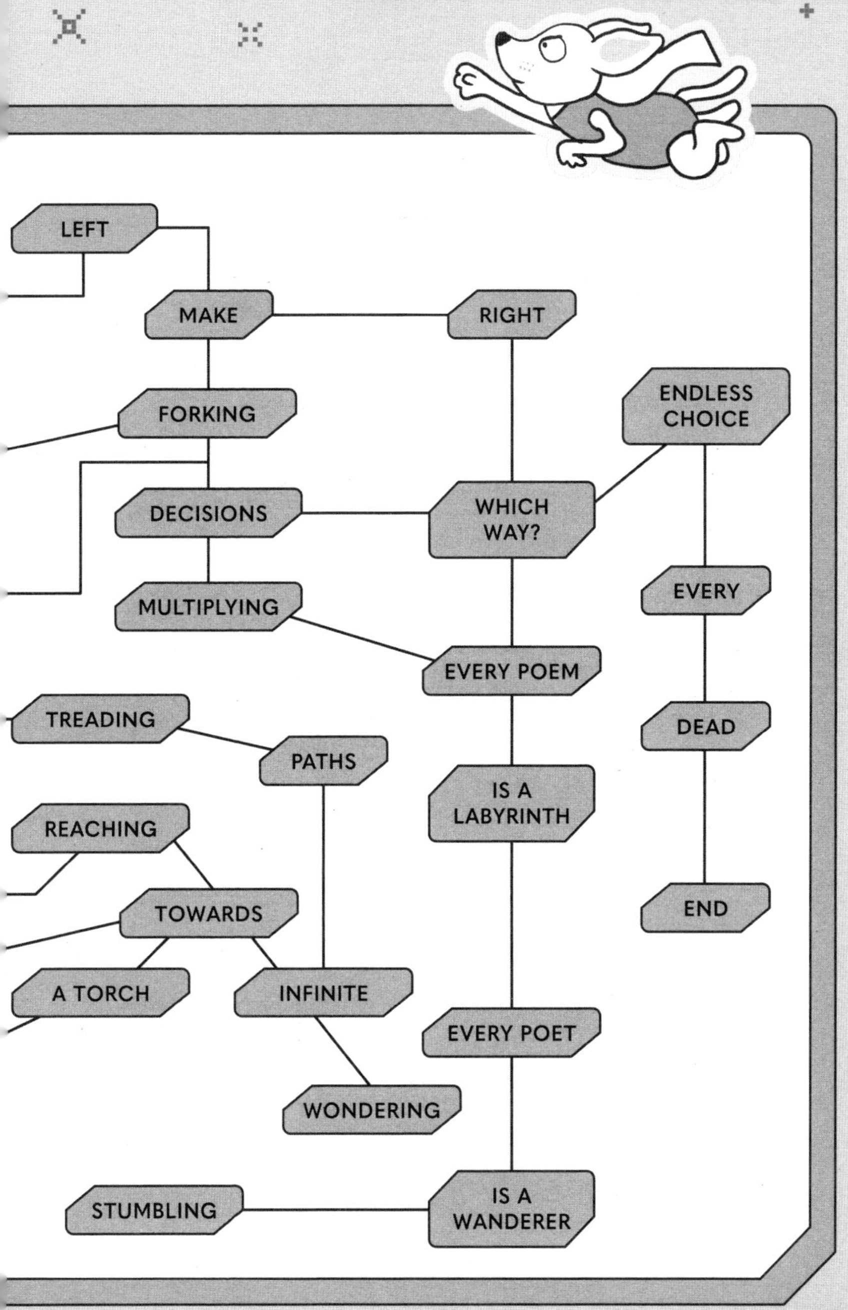
LEFT
MAKE
RIGHT
FORKING
ENDLESS CHOICE
DECISIONS
WHICH WAY?
EVERY
MULTIPLYING
EVERY POEM
TREADING
DEAD
PATHS
IS A LABYRINTH
REACHING
END
TOWARDS
A TORCH
INFINITE
EVERY POET
WONDERING
STUMBLING
IS A WANDERER

CHOOSE YOUR OWN POEM!

DECISION TREE SHEET

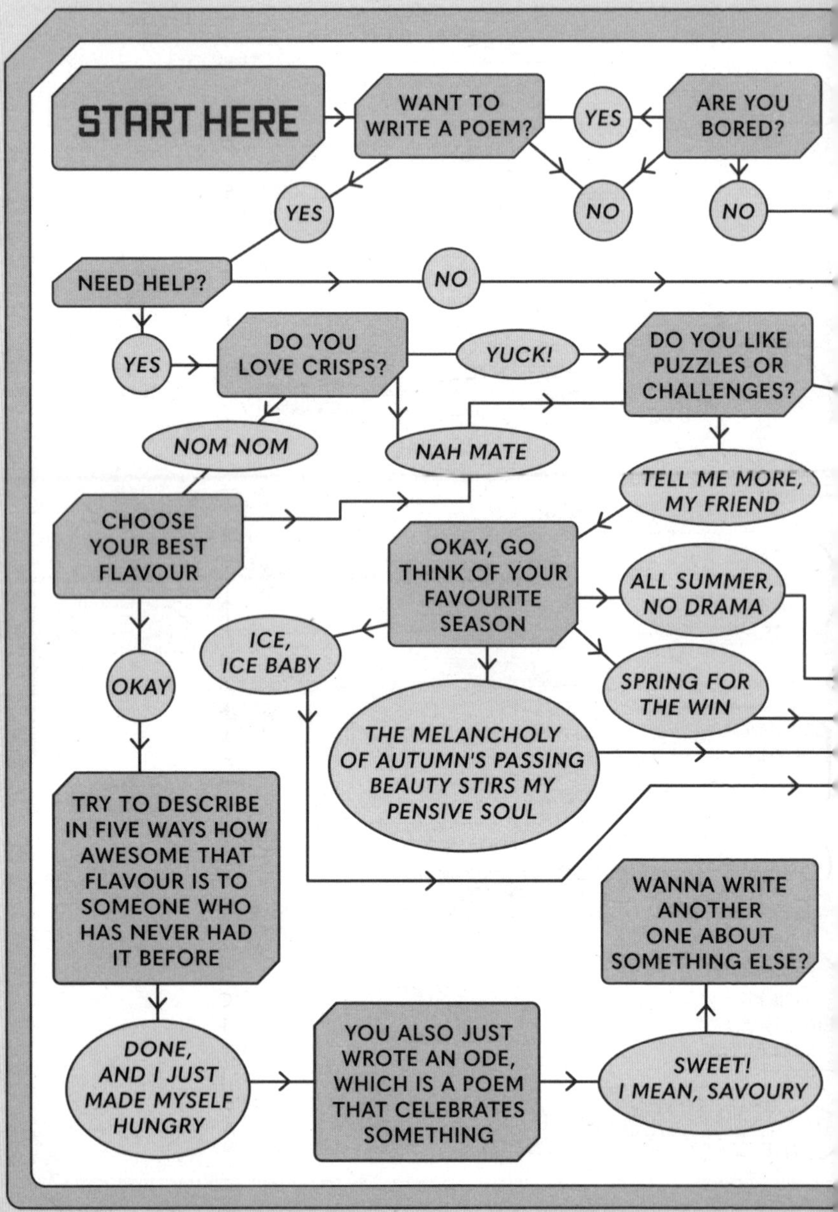
START HERE
WANT TO WRITE A POEM?
YES
ARE YOU BORED?
YES
NO
NO
NEED HELP?
NO
YES
DO YOU LOVE CRISPS?
YUCK!
DO YOU LIKE PUZZLES OR CHALLENGES?
NOM NOM
NAH MATE
TELL ME MORE, MY FRIEND
CHOOSE YOUR BEST FLAVOUR
OKAY, GO THINK OF YOUR FAVOURITE SEASON
ALL SUMMER, NO DRAMA
ICE, ICE BABY
SPRING FOR THE WIN
OKAY
THE MELANCHOLY OF AUTUMN'S PASSING BEAUTY STIRS MY PENSIVE SOUL
TRY TO DESCRIBE IN FIVE WAYS HOW AWESOME THAT FLAVOUR IS TO SOMEONE WHO HAS NEVER HAD IT BEFORE
WANNA WRITE ANOTHER ONE ABOUT SOMETHING ELSE?
DONE, AND I JUST MADE MYSELF HUNGRY
YOU ALSO JUST WROTE AN ODE, WHICH IS A POEM THAT CELEBRATES SOMETHING
SWEET! I MEAN, SAVOURY

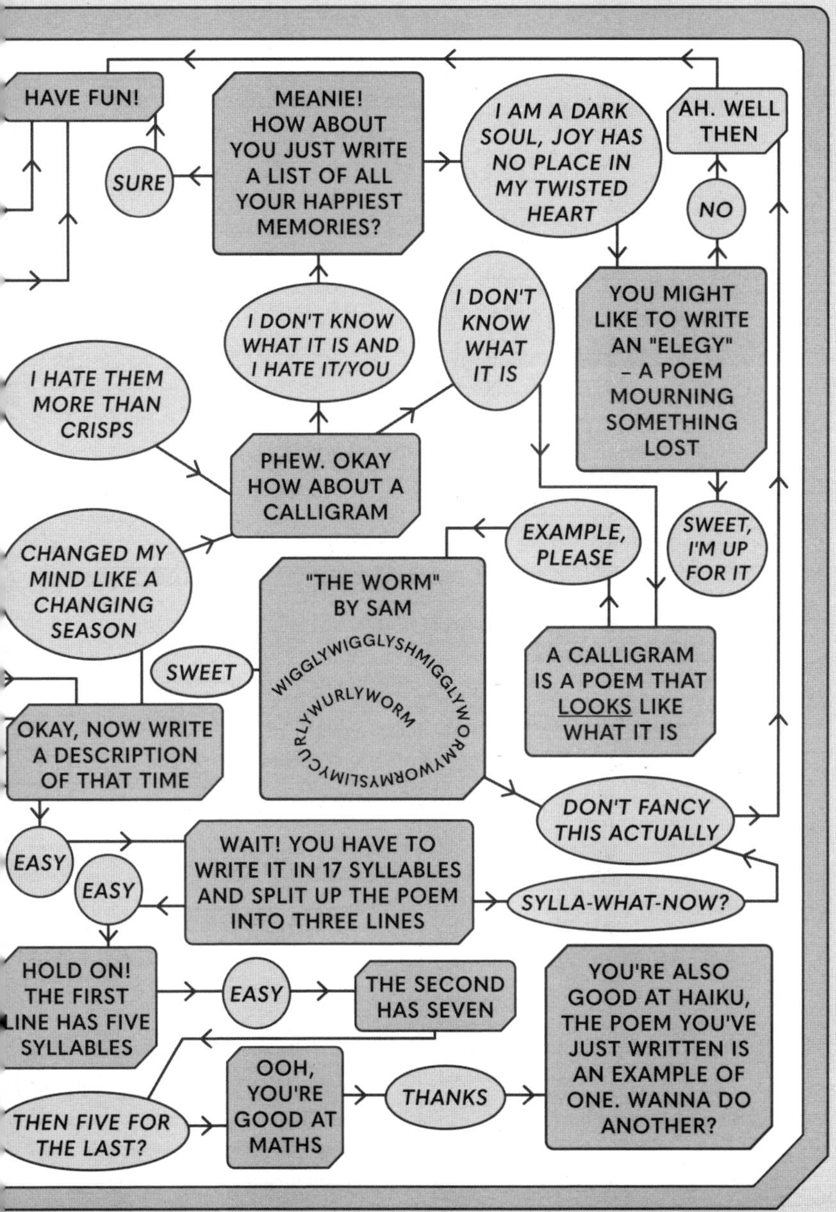
HAVE FUN!
SURE
MEANIE! HOW ABOUT YOU JUST WRITE A LIST OF ALL YOUR HAPPIEST MEMORIES?
I AM A DARK SOUL, JOY HAS NO PLACE IN MY TWISTED HEART
AH. WELL THEN
NO
I DON'T KNOW WHAT IT IS AND I HATE IT/YOU
I DON'T KNOW WHAT IT IS
YOU MIGHT LIKE TO WRITE AN "ELEGY" – A POEM MOURNING SOMETHING LOST
I HATE THEM MORE THAN CRISPS
PHEW. OKAY HOW ABOUT A CALLIGRAM
EXAMPLE, PLEASE
SWEET, I'M UP FOR IT
CHANGED MY MIND LIKE A CHANGING SEASON
"THE WORM" BY SAM
WIGGLYWIGGLYSHMIGGLYWORMYWORMYSLIMYCURLYWURLYWORM
SWEET
A CALLIGRAM IS A POEM THAT LOOKS LIKE WHAT IT IS
OKAY, NOW WRITE A DESCRIPTION OF THAT TIME
DON'T FANCY THIS ACTUALLY
EASY
EASY
WAIT! YOU HAVE TO WRITE IT IN 17 SYLLABLES AND SPLIT UP THE POEM INTO THREE LINES
SYLLA-WHAT-NOW?
HOLD ON! THE FIRST LINE HAS FIVE SYLLABLES
EASY
THE SECOND HAS SEVEN
YOU'RE ALSO GOOD AT HAIKU, THE POEM YOU'VE JUST WRITTEN IS AN EXAMPLE OF ONE. WANNA DO ANOTHER?
OOH, YOU'RE GOOD AT MATHS
THANKS
THEN FIVE FOR THE LAST?

POETS ARE ADVENTURERS

ADVENTURE SHEET

PICTURE OF YOUR INNER POET HERE

....

MY INVENTORY

STUFF I LIKE TO THINK ABOUT

MY BOOK OF SPELLS

FAVOURITE WORDS

....

....

....

....

....

....

....

....

SIMILES OF POWER

....

....

....

....

....

....

....

....

MY WEAPONS

STUFF YOU WANT TO PROTECT AND SAVE AND BELIEVE IN

THE SHINING SHIELD

STUFF YOU DON'T WANT IN YOUR POEMS

THE SWORD OF NO MERCY

MY HEALTH BAR

POETS CAN REST AND RELAX IF THEY FEEL LOW ON HEALTH

MY TREASURE TRACKER

REWARD YOURSELF EACH TIME YOU WRITE A POEM

MY QUEST

A MAP OF SOMEWHERE I'D LIKE TO GO OR SOMETHING I'D LIKE MY POEM TO DO

CHOOSE SOME POWERS

THE POWER TO:

- A) NOT RHYME
- B) BE SILLY
- C) SAY MY MIND
- D) NOT SHOW ANYONE MY POEMS

POETS ARE ADVENTURERS

poet are adventurers
into the realm of words
a land that can be silly,
sad, serious or absurd

each poem is a quest
to bring back something new
that treasure is your shiny,
gleaming, priceless
point of view

so use your words like spells of spelling
incant your inspirations
slay those inner demons
write righteous new creations

fill out this sheet first
before you start writing
good luck, adventurers!
safe trip and
happy smiting!

(SEE ADVENTURE SHEET)